The dark thing

Written by Kath Beattie
Illustrated by Alessandro Baldanzi

raintree
a Capstone company — publishers for children

Jack was off to the shop to get a can of corn for his mum.
"Go by the park," Mum said. 'I need to cook the dinner soon."

"But Chen said there is a dark thing in the park. A big, dark thing," said Jack. Mum said, "There is no dark thing in the park, Jack. Go and get the corn. Be as quick as you can."

Jack sat in the park. He had not got the can of corn yet.

"I will sit and look for the dark thing for a bit. Then I will get the corn," said Jack.

He waited and waited, but he did not see a dark thing. Jack looked under the big oak. He looked high up in the big oak. Then, a dark thing ran right by him. And then it ran right up the oak.

"The dark thing!" Jack yelled.
He ran off.
But then he said, "No, I will go back and look for the dark thing." So he ran back.

Jack looked up into the oak.
"It is so dark up there. I cannot see the dark thing at all," Jack said.
And then, there it was!

High up in the oak, the dark thing hid. It was hard to see it.

"You are big, your fur is dark and I think I see a long tail," said Jack.

"I think you are a panther!" Jack said. "A big, dark panther with long legs and big teeth."

Then Chen ran by.

"Jack," said Chen. "Do not sit in the park! Think of the dark thing."

"It is not a dark thing," Jack said. "It is a panther. It's up in this oak right now."

"A panther!" said Chen.
"Yes!" Jack said. "It has big teeth and long legs. Can you see it up there?"

Chen looked high up into the oak. "No. Wait! Yes, there it is!" he yelled.

Jack said, "I think it hissed at me as it ran by. Panthers do hiss."

"But," Chen said, "are there panthers in the park?"

"Yes!" said Jack. "I think it has got out of the zoo."

Chen said, "I do not think so. Did your mum tell you a panther had got out of the zoo?"

"No. Mum said there is no dark thing in the park. But there is! And it is a panther," Jack said.

Chen nodded. "Then let's ring the zoo to check," he said.

So Jack rang the zoo.

Jack was sad.
He said, "No luck. The zoo has no panthers, so it has not got out of there."
"See?" said Chen. "The dark thing is not a panther."
"Oh, well," said Jack. "I have to get a can of corn for dinner now."

"See you soon, then," said Chen.
Jack said, "Yes, see you soon."
But Jack was upset that Chen did not think the dark thing was a panther.

Mum was upset that Jack had been so long. "I needed to cook the corn sooner," she said.

She looked at Jack. "Did you sit in the park? Did you look for the dark thing?"

"Yes. And I met Chen," said Jack.

"I see," said Mum. "Did you and Chen see the dark thing?"

"Yes!" said Jack. "I think it is a panther."

"A panther!" said Mum. "Wow! I do not think so, Jack. Off you go and feed Hop-Hop."

Hop-Hop the rabbit was hopping in his big pen.

"There is a panther in the park," Jack said, feeding Hop-Hop a carrot.

Hop-Hop seemed to nod.

In the morning, Jack and Chen met in the park.
There was no panther high in the oak.
Jack said, "Hop-Hop thinks the dark thing is a panther."
Chen said, "I do not think it is a panther."

Jack said to Chen, "My dad said to me that a dark thing can be lots of things." "Oh, yes!" Chen said. "Lots of things." He hit Jack on the arm in fun. "I think the dark thing is a fox or a goat or a big, dark hen."

"Or a shark or a cow!" Jack yelled.
"Ha ha," Chen said. "Can a cow run up an oak?"
Jack said. "No, but I think a panther can run up high things."
"Let's check in a book," Chen said.

In Jack's room, they looked up panthers in a book.

"Oh," sighed Jack. "I think the dark thing might be too big to be a panther."

He said, "Let's look up things that hiss."

But it was not a thing that hissed.

Then Chen said, "Wait! Let's go back to the park. I need to have a look up that oak."

At the park, Chen said. "Jack, I think the sun has been fooling us."
Jack said, "How?"
"Things can look odd in the sunlight," Chen said. "Look in the oak!"
Jack looked. "Wow!" he said. "I see it now, too!"

"The sun **has** fooled us," Jack said. "The sun turned a pet cat into a long, dark panther! It was one big hoax!" Chen said, "That old sun had fun with us!" Jack let out a sad sigh. "Yes, but I do so wish it was a panther. A big, dark panther thing in the park."